HOW TO TRAIN A LAWYER

Ellen L. Hughes

The McKee Company
http://www.HowToTrainALawyer.com
P.O. Box 22996, Denver, CO 80222 U.S.A.
contact@themckeecompany.com
1-303-719-2154
Copyright ©2014 by The McKee Company
Ellen L. Hughes

For more resources, visit
www.HowToTrainALawyer.com

ISBN-13: 978-1-495352829

Disclaimer

The information contained herein should not be taken as a source of legal advice. The views expressed in this book and the website www.HowToTrainALawyer.com are those of the author alone. The author is not an attorney and has never practiced law.

ACKNOWLEDGEMENTS

The impetus for this book was my own personal injury which eventually morphed into this how-to book for people dealing with attorneys. Several people helped me through my recovery period and this book is dedicated to them.

Don, Susie and Donnie, Lori and Chris and Sissy and Mary, Christopher, Anna Lee, Meg, Bruce and Bonnie, Stevie, Uncle Clif, Aunt Evelyn and Uncle Carroll and Rags, the health providers at Denver Health and Hospitals, Swedish Medical Center and University of Colorado.

I would be remiss if I didn't mention the big guy in the sky. Thank you, God. Sorry for yelling at you so much, but I figured you could take it.

Ellen

PREFACE

A judge once said my father was so honest that he wouldn't even pick a nickel up off the street. My father was a lawyer. So was my uncle, my brother and my best friend's father. I grew up surrounded by decent, hard-working attorneys.

My career as a paralegal and legal assistant spanned 20+ years working with lawyers who treated clients with respect and clients reciprocated in kind. It was a good relationship. You might say I wore rose-colored glasses when it came to lawyers. In 2011 the glasses came off.

That year I suffered a major injury due to another person's negligence. In my quest for justice, I encountered incompetent, unprofessional, rude, bungling lawyers who made a bad situation worse.

Throughout this journey, I met people who related accounts of how they, too, had suffered at the hands of a lawyer;

they told stories of intimidation and manipulation. A common phrase echoed by many was, "I thought there was something wrong with me."

This opened my eyes. While I had spent years surrounded by honest lawyers, another faction had been growing; an unprincipled group more interested in feeding their ego and lining their pockets than in helping clients. Add the constant barrage of advertisements and it has become hard to tell the good attorneys from the bad.

People need to know which questions to ask when looking for an attorney. They need to grasp what to expect and request throughout the attorney/client relationship. Whereas most books in the legal field are written about law, **How To Train A Lawyer** is a book written about lawyers. It offers insight and logical, easy steps to build client confidence to help them deal effectively with lawyers.

CONTENTS

1

►CHOOSING AN ATTORNEY

1. Picking the right lawyer*

The most important thing is to hire an attorney who meets your legal and personal requirements. Ads on TV, radio, billboards and busses are good places to look for a restaurant, but not for an attorney. Advertising only proves the attorney has money to pay for it; not if they are the right attorney for you. Ask friends, family, and colleagues for referrals. Check with the local bar association; they may know attorneys who charge on a sliding scale.

*Even though the terms "lawyer" and "attorney" are used interchangeably in everyday conversation, technically a lawyer is trained in the law but has not necessarily passed the bar exam. An attorney is trained in law, passed the bar exam and admitted to practice law.

2.   Determine your needs

What are your personal preferences?

- Do you feel more comfortable with a man or a woman? *(There is no hard and fast rule for gender. There are tough men attorneys and mild-mannered female attorneys and vice versa..)*
- Do you prefer working with a younger or older person?
- How far are you willing to travel for appointments?
- How do you prefer to correspond: phone, e-mail, text or in person?
- How involved do you want to be?
- Do you prefer an attorney who is casual or formal? *(This refers to dress and/or language.)*

3. Your initial contact

During the selection process, your first contact can be by telephone. Ask questions to get a feel for their personality and how they work. Some questions to ask:

- Do you have experience with my type of case?
- If so, what is your success rate?

- What is your field of expertise?
- Do you have time to devote to my case?
- How do you prefer to communicate - phone calls, letters, text, e-mails?
- How promptly do you return calls and e-mails?
- Will you keep me regularly informed of actions taken in my case? How often?
- How do you charge - flat fee or contingency fee? (See #61)
- What is your attorney registration number? (*See #5*)

Even though an attorney may have worked on your type of case, it does not mean they are an expert. Their main expertise may be in another field but for various reasons (*help a friend, more income, required by firm to accept it*) took a case outside their normal field.

4. Reflect on the call
Immediately after the call, think about the conversation. How do you feel about the attorney? What is your

immediate reaction? Was it a good conversation? Ask yourself:

- Are they someone I would feel comfortable sharing intimate details of my life?
- Do I feel they will have my best interest at heart?
- Did they answer my questions so I could easily understand them?
- Did they seem to be organized?
- Do I feel they will respect me and my time?

If you answer "no" to any of the above, keep looking until you find one who comes across as confident and makes you feel comfortable.

5. Due diligence

Once you have found two, three or four attorneys that pass the first round, it's time to dig deeper. Using their name or registration number, check for any complaints lodged against them. Each state keeps records of complaints. Call your state bar association and ask where to find this information. For your convenience, *See Bonus Online Content.*

BONUS ONLINE CONTENT: Research an attorney's status and disciplinary history here: www.HowToTrainALawyer.com and click on Due Diligence on the bottom right.

If the attorney's record shows no history of grievances, it is time to set an appointment.

DO YOU REMEMBER?

1. Who has information on attorneys working on a sliding fee scale?

2. Where can you find if an attorney has a complaint filed against them?

3. Five questions to ask yourself to determine your personal preferences.

2

►THE INITIAL APPOINTMENT

6. Prepare for the appointment

Don't feel pressured to make a decision today. *The first meeting is a fact-finding mission.* It is for you to tell the attorney what you want and to determine if they can deliver it. Be as clear as you can when describing your needs.

- *I want a divorce and I want the house and the dog.*
- *I want to file a lawsuit for $50,000 for slander.*
- *I want a simple will drawn up within 30 days.*
- *I need a business contract between my partner and myself.*

Offer some specifics about your case so the attorney can make an informed assessment. Take your thoughts, and include feedback from people who

7

have your best interest at heart. (See #10 Take a friend) Compile it in logical order. Make sure to **answer the 5 W's - Who, What, When, Where and Why.** A construction defect case may look like this:

Who: Contractor's Name
What: I want to sue the Contractor for $_____ because the new siding started pulling away from the house and exposed the interior of the house to the elements. The cost of the siding was $_____ and items inside the house were damaged.
When: Noticed the damage inside within 3 months of installation.
Where: My house at 123 Main Street.
Why: I want to sue to get money to fix the problem and cover household items ruined by the defective siding.

This way you your attorney will get a complete understanding of what you want and why you want it.

7. Make a good first impression
Many attorneys offer a free initial consultation. Schedule at a time

convenient for you. Arrive on time, bring your list (*See #6*) and any pertinent legal and personal documentation. Don't bring children or pets. Bring a picture ID. Call ahead to ask about parking. Dress appropriately. If you aren't sure what to wear, ask. Dressing in ripped, dirty clothes or looking like you just rolled out of bed sends a message that you aren't serious about your case. If you don't think it's important, why should anyone else?

8. Ask a lot of questions
Determine if the lawyer is in line with what you want. Asking questions will give you important insight.

- What is the best case scenario?
- What is the worst case scenario?
- What is a realistic outcome?
- Would you pursue this if you were me? Why or why not?
- Is this region sympathetic to my type of case? (See #60)
- What is a reasonable amount of time and costs I should expect?

When deciding questions to ask, use the basic Who, What, When, Where and Why. If you want a simple will and want it completed within a month, ask them what they would charge and if they could do it in that time frame. (*I know clients who waited a year for their simple wills.*) Your questions will depend on the legal matter. Is there a deadline involved? Do you want specific restitution? Let the attorney know all pertinent information. When they know your expectations, they may give you other options you hadn't considered.

9. Listen to <u>how</u> an attorney talks
- Are their answers hard to follow?
- Do they use legal jargon?
- Do they answer a question with a question?
- Do they change the subject?
- Do they brag or oversell their services?

These are red flags. If they evade questions in the first meeting, what is going to happen down the road?

There are times when a client asks a question and the attorney responds by assigning them busywork to the point they are too overwhelmed to think about what the attorney is doing - or not doing. Avoid this kind of attorney.

10. Intimidation factor

Attorneys can be intimidating and people may feel pressured to hire the first one. Don't. The first meeting is a fact-finding mission. While they are assessing your case, you should be assessing them. Meet at least two attorneys before making a decision. Take notes and review them later when you are more relaxed.

11. Trust your instincts

This meeting is to determine if you can work with the attorney. If you feel tension or something doesn't feel right, thank the attorney for their time, let them know you will think about it and get back to them. As soon as possible, (*preferably the same day*) let them know you won't need their services.

12. Take a friend

This is smart, especially if you are feeling ill, on medication, or just out of sorts. A second person may catch things you miss or think of other questions to ask. Compare notes afterwards.

If you feel the attorney is the right one and want to hire them on the spot, ask to confer with your friend in private before making a decision.

13. The waiting room

If your appointment is scheduled for 10:30 and you are left cooling your heels until 11:00, that tells you a few things about the attorney: 1) They don't value your time, 2) Aren't organized, or 3) Overbook clients. This is not a good way to start a relationship. If they apologize for the delay and give a believable explanation, give them another chance. If no reason is offered, move on to the next name on your list.

14. A revolving door

If you interview an attorney who can't seem to keep assistants, take heed. An office in a constant state of flux speaks volumes - none of it good. Not only does it point out possible problems, (*caused by the common denominator - most likely the lawyer*) but the very organization of the office (*including your file*) will be affected. (*I know an attorney who went through five paralegals in one year!*) Who suffers most when this happens? The client!

You can easily find out how long someone has worked there. Ask them.

DO YOU REMEMBER?

1. What are four of your responsibilities for your first appointment?

2. Why should you take someone else with you to appointments?

3. Why should you listen to how an attorney talks and not just what they say?

6. How long should you wait after the first meeting to let an attorney know you don't need their services?

3

►THE HIRING PROCESS

You found an attorney who seems to fit your needs. Now what? Open communication is the key.

15. Discuss your expectations

You have already made your basic needs known. Now it is time to give details. The lawyer is not a mind reader; give them as much information as possible. Let them know what you expect - not only the outcome of your case, but how you want to be treated. What level of service do you expect? How often do you want updates? The Client Constitution covers billing, communication, and personnel issues which you should discuss before hiring any attorney.

16. Client Constitution

Review it thoroughly and choose points that are important to you. Discuss them with your lawyer. Make sure they agree to your requests. If they don't agree with something that is important to you, find one who will.

The Client Constitution

- Client prefers to communicate with the same personnel throughout the case.
- If staffing changes occur, Client will not pay for time educating new attorneys/staff about the case.
- Client will be kept current on case developments in a timely manner.
- Client will be copied on all court-filed documents in a timely manner.
- Client will be copied on all correspondence in relation to case.
- Client will be provided a schedule in advance of all court-appointed due dates (*depositions, discovery, etc.*).
- Client shall receive copies of invoices/receipts for items charged

by outside vendors (*copies, postage, private investigator, etc.*).

- Before incurring any expense over $_____ (*not less than $25*), Client will be notified for approval.
- Before ordering medical or other records, attorney will verify if there is insurance or other asset to cover the cost. (See #58)
- Before dismissing a case, attorney will notify Client.
- Hourly rates may not be increased without prior Client approval.
- Client will receive a monthly statement detailing description, timekeeper, time and costs.
- Client shall receive copies of invoices/receipts for items charged by outside vendors (*copies, postage, private investigator, etc.*).
- Amounts submitted by outside vendors will be charged to Client at face value.
- Client will receive prompt follow-up to all communications to attorney and staff.
- Client expects efficient, timely completion of work, including

keeping Client file current and in good order.

- Meetings are held during regular office hours unless cleared in advance with Client.
- Only one lawyer/staff member will attend meetings, hearings or other matters on Client's behalf.
- Attorney in charge will avoid:
  o Overstaffing
  o Frequent shuffling of assigned personnel
  o Extensive "rework" of a written work product
  o Handling specific tasks by persons who are either overqualified or underqualified
  o Review of documents by multiple timekeepers
  o Performing premature or minor legal or factual research
- Client will not be billed for:
  o Internal conferences
  o Internal notes or memorandum
  o Scheduling meetings or depositions

o Research regarding simple issues which should already be within the knowledge of the firm

o Timekeeping (billing for time it takes to create the bill)

 BONUS ONLINE CONTENT: Download your own copy of the Client Constitution at HowToTrainALawyer.com

Once you have discussed the Client Constitution with your attorney, record that it has been discussed. If possible, have the attorney sign a copy. Send a copy of it to them, with a short cover letter/email, *"I am sending you a copy of the Client Constitution that we discussed on (date)"*. Keep a copy of both for your files.

Do you feel like you are overstepping your authority by telling your attorney what you expect? Don't. There is nothing in the Client Constitution that demands too much or is out of line with what a client should expect from their attorney. Corporations do it all the time. It's just good business.

Agreeing upon these issues at the beginning increases your odds of having a harmonious relationship with your attorney.

17. Business Owners

The Client Constitution is suitable for individuals and companies. However, there are additional points that apply more specifically to business owners or clients with action-intensive cases.

- Messenger services should be provided at cost and used only when an alternative is unavailable.
- Express mail should be provided at cost and used only when an alternate service is not available.
- Client needs to approve all travel expenses in advance.
- No local travel expenses (*within 100 miles of firm's office*) will be reimbursed.
- Photocopying (in-house) may not exceed .15/page. If there is a large volume of documents, Client shall be given the opportunity to copy the documents.

18. Level of involvement

No one has a more vested interest in your case than you. *Decide how hands-on you want to be.* At one end of the spectrum you can be very involved and offer to do research and legwork that doesn't require legal training. *(This level of involvement is usually allowed only by small firms or sole attorney.)* On the opposite end, you can take a *laissez faire* approach and let the attorney and staff do all the work.

At the very minimum, you should keep all paperwork organized in one place so you can easily find any document. An expandable file folder works well. It is also good to track due dates on a calendar so you know the deadlines. No matter what level of involvement you choose, don't overstep your authority or become a nuisance. **When in doubt, ask your attorney.**

19. Fee agreement

Once you decide on a lawyer, they will give you a fee agreement to sign. (*See #52*) <u>Read it carefully</u>. It is a contract that covers the terms of what the attorney offers to do for you, payment and your acceptance of the terms. It is signed by both parties.

Depending on the type of case and how detailed the agreement, (*See #61*) it may describe how fees will be set, what expenses will be paid, estimate of fees, deposit of funds, how withdrawals from a trust account will be made and how the funds will be replenished, if a retainer fee is required and what happens when that money runs out. In a contingency case, it will specify the attorney's percentage and when fees will be calculated.

 BONUS ONLINE CONTENT: Review examples of different types of fee agreements at HowToTrainALawyer.com

DO YOU REMEMBER?

1. Who signs the fee agreement?

2. What is the minimum you should do for your case?

3. Why you should want to be involved in your case?

4. What are the points in the Client Constitution that are important to you?

5. How can you record the fact that you have discussed the Client Constitution with the attorney?

4

►WORK WITH AN ATTORNEY

You have hired an attorney who meets your requirements. Now it's time to talk about what they expect from you.

20. Client responsibilities

Do:
- Respond to all communication from attorney in a timely manner.
- Keep messages short and to the point.
- Dress appropriately for all meetings and/or court dates.
- Tell your attorney everything and do not lie.
- Review all documents your attorney gives you.
- Keep all paperwork organized.
- Keep a record of documents you give to attorney.

- Make sure your attorney has your current contact information.
- Provide copies of all documents your attorney requests and <u>keep the originals</u>.
- Pay your bill on time.
- Let your attorney know as soon as possible if you will be late or cannot make an appointment.

Do Not:

- Leave repeated messages about the same issue.
- Leave several messages throughout the day (*unless it is an emergency*). If you have several questions, consolidate them into one message.
- Show up at the office without an appointment.
- Bring children or pets to meetings.
- Get involved personally with your attorney.
- Contact witnesses or others involved in your case without first informing attorney.

In addition to these rules, teat your attorney as you want to be treated - with respect and common courtesy.

21. Respect staff and their time

Employees are an important part of the legal team. A client usually talks to the staff more often than with the attorney. If you have a legal question, speak to the attorney. If you need documents or a question that doesn't require legal expertise, speak to a staff member. Show the staff the same courtesy and respect as you do the lawyer. Do not leave multiple messages regarding the same issue, keep to the point and be polite.

22. How you can help

Depending on your desired level of involvement, your comfort level and the agreement you have with your attorney, you can assist in several ways.

- **Offer to do research** that does not require legal training. A lot of it can be done on the internet. (*See #67*)

- **Pick up and deliver** documents or copy jobs, especially if they are needed immediately. It can save the rush fee (*which you ultimately pay*).
- **Obtain contact information** for friends and family who are potential witnesses. ***Inform the attorney before you do this*** in case they have already contacted them or have a reason for you not to contact a person.

Small firms and sole practitioners are more open to client involvement than a larger firm. Whatever assistance you offer, keep a record of your actions with as many details as possible. (*See #66*)

23. Inside an attorney's mind

What make an attorney an attorney? Wouldn't it be helpful to know how they think? If you knew that, it might make it easier to understand their actions. In her book, *Lawyer, Know Thyself*, Susan Daicoff discusses the personality traits of an attorney:

"Individuals who choose to enter law school seem to generally share the following characteristics as children: They are highly focused on academics, have greater needs for dominance, leadership and attention and they prefer initiating activity...It was found, in a comparative study, that concern for emotional suffering and for the feelings of others tended to be less emphasized than in the childhood homes of dental or social work students."

In short - they are logical, focused, like to be in charge, and seek attention.

Like Spock from Star Trek, attorneys can be perceived as cold and unemotional. They are logical. They deal with facts. They do not deal well with people who are emotional.

24. Get your point across

When talking with an attorney, it may appear they are so focused on what they are saying, they *don't hear you*. If you have something to say, wait for a break then get their attention. Look

them in the eye, clear your throat, tap
a pencil - anything to make them focus
on what you are saying. Remember,
lawyers love to talk so let them - to a
point - but be vigilant and say what
you need to say. If they charge by the
hour, guide them back to the topic as
soon as possible.

25. Confidence builders

There are many easy ways to build up
your confidence so you feel more in
control.

- Imagine wearing a Superman cape
  on your back or having a crown or
  tiara on your head. It may sound
  silly, but these mental images can
  make you feel and act powerful and
  important. Prefer another image?
  Choose one that makes you feel
  strong.

- Present yourself as a professional.
  The cost of your outfit is not
  important; what is important is that
  your clothes, hair, nails and shoes
  all reflect that you think of yourself
  as a winner.

•Increase your energy. K-27 is the 27th pair of acupressure points on the kidney meridian. By tapping on these points, you will feel more alert. Place your fingers on your collarbone, slide them toward the center and find the bumps where they stop. Drop about an inch beneath these corners and slightly outward. Most people have a slight indent here. Using your fingers, gently tap or massage these points while breathing deeply (*in through the nose and out through the mouth*) for about 20 seconds. This will make your energy flow in the right direction and help you think more clearly.

•Increase your personal space. Instead of keeping your body and belongings directly in front of you, spread out a little bit. Without being overly dramatic, drape an arm over the chair next to you. Place your belongings on the table instead of on the floor. Take up a little more space (*not a lot*) than you normally would. Try this at a restaurant, first with keeping everything close together and then spread out a little bit and notice the difference in how the wait staff treats you. This has been tested and people who take up more space are perceived as being more important and treated accordingly.

- Keep eye contact. One of the first signs that people are nervous is they find it hard to maintain eye contact. They look at the floor, their hands, the table, anywhere but the person talking to them. Start practicing so you can look the lawyer in the eyes and not flinch. Don't stare, but smile, blink and pay attention to what they are saying. You will come across as confident.

26. Control or manipulation?
Attorneys like to be in control. That is a good thing. You want one who is in control; someone who will take charge and guide the outcome to benefit you. It is when they try to manipulate you that problems arise. They may ask a

question in such a way (*like a salesman*) that you feel obligated to give a specific answer. Or perhaps they ask you to do something you consider unreasonable. If you feel this happening, ask yourself:

- Will this help my case?
- Is this in line with what we agreed upon in the Client Constitution?
- What would happen if I do or don't do this?
- Are there other options available?

Review the options and if you still feel it is not in your best interest to do what they are asking, tell them the issue has been addressed and there will be no further discussion on this point unless they offer some new information.

DO YOU REMEMBER?

1. What are five responsibilities of the client?

2. Should you give the attorney your original documents or copies?

3. What are different ways you can help with your cases?

4. What are four characteristics of an attorney?

5. What should you do if you feel you are being manipulated?

5

►ENDING THE ATTORNEY/ CLIENT RELATIONSHIP

When all is said and done, hopefully everyone walks away happy. You have your desired outcome and the attorney gets paid. Wrapping up is fairly simple. The attorney should give you a document outlining any final matters they need to take care of and/or any action you need to take.

But what if it doesn't end well or you feel you need to get a new attorney? Does the thought of firing an attorney scare you? It shouldn't. If you hired a plumber and he didn't show up for two weeks, you would have no problem firing them. Firing a lawyer is no different. However, there are a few more things to consider before giving them the pink slip.

27. Talk with them

Before terminating your attorney's services, it is in your best interest to talk with them. If you think they aren't giving your case their full attention, talk to them about it. It may be simple miscommunication. If the problem appears to be overbilling, it could be an accounting error. Try to give them the benefit of the doubt. A 10-minute phone call can save you a lot of time and headaches.

28. Timing is everything

You can change attorneys at any time. Before you do consider what is best for your case. Changing lawyers may delay your case. If you feel you must get new counsel, do it as soon as possible. If you wait until just before trial or some other deadline, it may be hard to find an attorney willing to take over at that late date.

29. Attorney action/inaction

Do you feel your attorney has lost interest in your case? Are they not returning phone calls or not keeping you up to date? (*They did agree to the*

Client Constitution, right?) Before firing them, express your concerns by sending a simple, factual, non-emotional letter. If they don't respond or address your issues satisfactorily, then it is time to sever ties.

30. Get a second opinion
If you feel the problem is deeper than a personality conflict or simple disagreement, talk to someone. **Do not mention your attorney's name** or information that would make it easy to guess their identity. You could be opening yourself up for a defamation lawsuit. Consider talking to another attorney. Give them the bare bones description, no details. Ask them to evaluate your attorney's actions.

31. Contact local bar association
Another place to go is the local bar association. Without revealing your lawyer's name, relate your situation. They will not give legal advice, but they can let you know if your attorney's actions are problematic.

32. Personal reasons

Maybe you want to stop the action due to personal reasons: You decide not to sell your business, you and your spouse kiss and make up, the lawsuit is taking over your life. Whatever the reason, you made a decision to stop. Just make sure it is in your best interest and no one is forcing the decision on you.

33. Drop or postpone?

If your case involves a lawsuit, get your attorney's opinion on how the case is progressing and any possible options before you drop it. Check the statute of limitations in your state in case you may want to re-file at a later date. (*See #54*)

34. You are entitled to your file

You have decided to sever ties with your attorney. What should you reasonably expect? First, you are entitled to a copy of your file *minus work product.* Work product consists of conversations with a client or witness, research conducted, attorney notes, writings, and other confidential materials. If depositions were taken, you would receive copies if and when you paid for them.

The attorney may charge to copy your file. Review your fee agreement for details regarding your file. Since you should have been copied on documents filed with the court and all correspondence, the actual number of documents you actually need may be few.

35. Monies due to you

If a retainer was paid, the balance should be returned to you with your file or soon thereafter. The refund should include an overview of total fees and costs. (*You should have received detailed monthly statements.*) If you owe money, the attorney should release your file after payment is made.

36. Arbitration

For major issues such as overbilling, you can request arbitration where parties bring their dispute before a neutral third-party, an arbitrator.

They are often former judges or experienced attorneys. Once both parties have presented their evidence, the arbitrator issues a decision. Arbitration decisions are generally binding and legally enforceable, but must be confirmed by a court. This can save you time, money and headaches.

 BONUS ONLINE CONTENT: If you have decided to file a grievance against your attorney, visit HowToTrainALawyer.com.

37. When to report an attorney

Missing deadlines, failing to advise you about court dates or suggesting you lie are considered unethical conduct and should be reported. Other examples of conduct that may be cause for discipline are:

• They represent the other party, whether in your case or another

• Misrepresent whether or not they have taken certain actions

• Will not provide a complete written

accounting for money due you or money they are holding on your behalf

•Settle your case without your permission and nothing in the fee agreement authorizes them to do so

To file a grievance, contact your state bar. For grievance information, visit www.HowToTrainALawyer.com.

38. Filing a grievance

When filing a grievance, be certain of the facts. You need proof; gut feelings or intuition won't stand up in court. You must be able to provide evidence, either with documentation or reliable witnesses. Filing a grievance does not guarantee the attorney will be sanctioned but it should at least make someone should sit up and take notice.

DO YOU REMEMBER?

1. After ending your case, do you have to pay to get your file?

2. Why should you not mention your attorney's name when talking to others about their actions?

3. What are five things a lawyer may do that can be considered unethical?

4. What could happen if you change attorneys within weeks of your trial?

6

►TO-DO LIST

The key is to leave a paper trail. The more documentation and details, the better. Be thorough. You don't know what will be the "smoking gun" that could make or break your case.

39. The devil is in the details
The length of your list depends on your legal matter. If you want a business contract drawn up, the list will be short. If you were injured in a car accident and are seeking restitution, your list may seem never-ending. *The following list is geared toward a full-blown personal injury lawsuit and is extensive. If your matter is more simple, follow the steps that apply.*

40. Keep a diary

Start a diary as soon as possible. The longer you put it off, the more details you forget. If you aren't able to write or type, have someone else write it or record it and have it transcribed later.

Start your diary with a complete narrative of the incident. List as many details as you can remember.

▶ date
▶ location *(address and description)*
▶ people/animals description of all involved
▶ contact information of witnesses
▶ vehicle license plate, signage, bumper stickers, condition, etc.
▶ time of day
▶ weather conditions

Once you start your diary, **keep it current.** *Enter notes on everything, whether or not you think it is important.* You can determine later what is pertinent to your case. What should you write in your diary? Your conversations, thoughts, and actions.

Conversations

Any time you talk with anyone involved with the incident, record the following:

▶ First and last name of participants
▶ Person's occupation and/or relationship to your case *(medical provider, witness)*
▶ Complete contact information *(name, phone, address, e-mail)*
▶ Date
▶ Time and duration *(include a.m. or p.m.)*
▶ Location *(via telephone, e-mail, or if in person, address)*
▶ Subject of conversation *(include details and direct quotes when possible)*

You want to paint a vivid picture so include as many details as possible.

Thoughts

Keep track of your feelings.
▶ Your mood *(happy, depressed, angry)*
▶ What caused you to feel this way *(Sad because I cannot attend a*

wedding due to my injuries, afraid because I cannot pay my bills)

You want people to understand your frame of mind.

Actions
Keep track of your day-to-day life and how it has changed.

▶ Events that are a direct result of the incident (*doctor appointments*)

▶ Things you cannot do any more (*morning walks, laundry, mowing*)

▶ How your injuries affect daily life (*can't sit for long periods of time*)

Show specifically how your life changed as a direct result of the incident.

41. Contact list
Keep contact information together. Some information may already be in your diary but also keep a separate file. It will be easier to retrieve quickly. *Group your contacts according to their relationship to your case -* medical providers, witnesses, etc. For people you contact often, store their

number in your phone or on speed dial. Anything that saves you time, saves your sanity. **Keep this list current.**

Include assistants and support staff in your contact list. They can be invaluable. When an attorney, doctor or other professional is unavailable, the assistant may be able to locate them or answer your question.

Each contact should include:

Name
Telephone (Main)
Telephone (Other)
Street Address
Mailing Address
Email
Company
Occupation (*doctor or assistant, lawyer or paralegal, etc.*)
Relationship to case (*health provider, witness, etc.*)
Hours/Days they are available
Comments

42. Record your impressions

Get in the habit of recording your _impression_ of a person. Notes like "helpful" or "had an accident similar to mine" will come in handy if you need to contact them again. It helps you establish rapport and they will be more inclined to help you. If you felt they could not help or were not the right person to talk to, make a note so you will not waste your time with them again. *The more you record, the fewer things you have to remember.*

43. Calendar future dates

A diary keeps track of the past; a calendar keeps track of the future. For example, on your calendar you might write, "If I have not heard from Mr. Jones by today, send Letter #2" (*See #49*). "If I have not received report by today, contact attorney."

Attorneys keep track of due dates with a process called "calendaring". Ask your attorney to share important dates with you so you can **record them on your calendar**. This may seem unnecessary, especially if you don't want to be kept in the loop. But there have been cases where attorneys missed deadlines for deposition and/or filing documents with the court.

These errors negatively impacted the case. If a due date is approaching and you haven't received notice that action has been taken, call your attorney and ask for a status report.

44. Track loss of income

Your attorney should provide you with a log to keep track of income and expenses. Unfortunately, that doesn't always happen. In the end, it is up to you to **keep records**. If you missed work due to injuries, keep a record of your days absent. If you are employed by someone, it is easy to keep track of missed work.

If you are self-employed, get in the habit of keeping detailed information regarding your business schedule. Did you miss a meeting due to a conflicting doctor appointment? Were you unable to give a seminar that could have brought in revenue? Make a note of it.

As with the contact list, this information will be in your diary. But *keep a separate log strictly for lost income* because it will be easier to find this information when needed. A simple table like the one below is sufficient.

Date	Income	Reason
		Why opportunity to make money was lost

45. Keep all receipts
Medical and legal expenses are easy to remember, but expand your thinking. If an injury prevents you from performing some task, keep track of money you paid to get it done (*mowing, cleaning, laundry, etc.*). Did you chug Pepto Bismol because of stress caused by the incident? Could you not use your paid gym membership due to your injuries? Keep a running total so it will be easy to know your out-of-pocket expenses at

a glance. If the receipt doesn't include a description, write it on the receipt. Your expense log might look like this:

Date	Amount	Payee and Description
1/2/12	$15.45	CVS - Antibiotics
1/2/12	$ 1.80	Postage - signed documents to attorney
1/4/12	$ 8.25	15 miles - Round trip to doctor

46. Keep track of communication

In addition to daily events in your diary, keep records of any communication regarding the incident. This includes telephone calls, e-mails, letters and in-person conversations. Also keep copies of any attachments.

>**Telephone calls** are easy to track, especially if made on a cell phone. Make a note of the day and time, who you talked to and the subject of the call. A detailed diary holds a lot of weight in court. Recording a

conversation can be done, but check the law. Each state has wiretapping laws and rules on consent of the parties. When you make or receive a phone call, follow it up with something written that reiterates what was said. It can be as simple as a short e-mail: *"As we discussed on the phone today, you will send me your findings on Mr. Smith by Wednesday, the 23rd."*

>Written correspondence leaves a paper trail and is important to a lawsuit. Keep signed copies of all letters you send and receive, *along with any attachments.* Most letters may be sent via U.S. Mail. If you are sending something that requires an answer or contains original documents, **require the recipient sign for it**. Many private delivery companies offer this service (FedEx, UPS). The U.S. Post Office offers Certified Mail with Return Receipt Requested. This also allows you to track the package and know when it is delivered and who signed for it.

47. Basic communication rules

Include your contact information on everything. The placement doesn't matter - it can be at the top in the letterhead or under your signature. This applies to all forms of communication. Include a subject line that provides enough details to determine the matter at a glance. Details may include name, account or case number, date of loss and name of defendant.

Name
Address
City, State and Zip Code
Email Address
Phone Number(s)
Date

Address

Re: Your Name
      Case No.: 12345
      Date of Loss: 7/26/11
      Defendant: Individual's Name

Dear (Mr./Mrs. Name or Sir/Madam):

Body of letter

Sincerely,

Your Name
(If you prefer, list contact details here instead of at the top in the letterhead.)

Enclosures - *List all enclosures*
cc: *List all who are receiving copy*

48. Tracking e-mails

When sending an e-mail, copy yourself so you have a dated copy for your files. Every time you send an email, *change the subject line to reflect the content.* For instance, if a private investigator emails you and asks if you want them to check out Mr. Smith, when you reply, change the subject line to "Answer to question regarding Mr. Smith. When the content of an email is clearly defined in the subject line, it is easy to find a specific email.

For an easy way to remember the above, follow these guidelines:

TO:	*Save all addresses and note how the recipient is related to your case*
CC:	*If you have more than one contact at a company, cc all contacts to cover all bases*
SUBJECT:	*Change subject to reflect the content of current email*

49. Mass produce communication

Usually the lawyer will communicate with companies, but if you are dealing with companies before hiring a lawyer, there are some things you can do to make it easier on yourself. If there is someone who you think may be hard to deal with (*insurance companies are a prime example*), **write several letters at one time**. If they don't take action after one letter, you already have another ready to send. This saves time and frustration. Write two, three, even four letters at one time, making minor changes in each letter. The first paragraph should refer to previous letters:

"I am writing because I have not received a response to my letter of January 31, 2012."

Simply cut and paste the majority of the previous letter. If you are corresponding by e-mail, use the prior e-mail to create a new one, and make reference to the previous email.

50. Clearly state what you want

In all correspondence, state the facts clearly and succinctly. Do not be emotional. Do not use profanity. Write as if you were not involved and merely reporting what happened. Instead of "That rude employee said he would send me the paperwork but didn't," write, "*I am still waiting to receive the paperwork Mr. Jones promised to send when I talked to him at 2:15 p.m. on May 15.*"

51. Give them time to reply

Send the first letter and if they do not take action, send out the next letter. How long should you wait? Use your judgment. You don't want them to forget about you but you also don't want to come across as a stalker. A good rule of thumb - *If you haven't received a response within two weeks, send the next letter.*

52. Taking it to the next level

What if you don't get a response? Go up the chain of command. Give people two chances to reply. Then contact their supervisor. If you still don't get satisfaction, contact someone above them. And so on. If you have to go to the top and contact the head of the company, so be it. They won't be happy and will want the situation handled quickly. (*You may want to go directly to the owner of the company. Saves a lot of time.*)

DO YOU REMEMBER?

1. List five things on your to-do list.

2. When should you require a delivery?

3. How long should you wait before sending a follow-up letter?

4. When a lawyer "calendars", what type of information does it contain?

5. Why should you keep separate contact and income logs?

6. What should you do if a receipt doesn't have a description on it?

7. What three types of things should you track in your diary?

8. Your contact information should include five items. Name them.

7

►THE BASICS

While behavior varies from attorney to attorney and case to case, there are basic fundamentals that apply across the board. *Learn and understand* these and you will save time and money. *Follow* them and you will be your own best advocate.

53. Keep your eyes on the prize

Always have your goal in mind. If you want to file a lawsuit for $5,000 and the attorney's fees will run that much or more, it's time to walk away. Do you need a simple will with no property or assets? The cost and time to have this prepared should be minimal. When determining whether to go ahead with a legal matter, consider how much money and time you are willing to spend and is it worth the aggravation?

54. Statute of limitations

Maybe you're undecided if you want to go forward with your case. Perhaps you want to wait a while until you feel better. There are many reasons to put things on hold; just be aware there is a deadline for filing a lawsuit known as the statute of limitations. For personal injury cases, this can run anywhere from one to six years from the date of the incident; for property damage it is one to ten years. Each state sets their own time limit. Check your state's deadlines and file before the deadline.

55. Plan for the worst, hope for the best

Assume nothing will be easy. Act as if you are dealing with the government or large company. Some people will argue that negative thinking is wrong. I say it is just being practical. If you think everything will go smoothly and it does not, it makes it harder to rally yourself after a letdown. If you expect it is going to be an uphill battle, you steel yourself against adversity. Then even the smallest triumph makes you feel like a winner.

56. Defendant has no insurance

What if the person responsible for your loss has no insurance or personal assets to attach? Personal injury attorneys work almost exclusively on cases that have a pot at the end of the rainbow. No rainbow. No pot. No case. Advertisements portraying altruistic lawyers show only part of the picture. For lawyers to truly care, *there has to be money to make it worth their time*. Nothing personal, just business.

57. Have a realistic timeline

Television attorneys wrap up a case in 60 minutes. Real lawyers working real cases **can take years**. The discovery alone (*taking depositions, answering interrogatories , obtaining medical records,*) can take months, even years. Lawsuits for personal injury cases may not be filed until an expert has declared the person to be at Maximum Medical Improvement (MMI).

For non-litigious matters such as a patent search or estate planning, the timeline is much shorter. Ask your attorney how many hours they anticipate it will take. *You play an important role here.* The quicker you provide information, the faster the attorney can complete the work.

58. Wait to order medical records

Tell your attorney to verify the availability of insurance or assets before ordering medical records or other reports. These documents are paid out of monies awarded to you. Records, especially medical records, can cost thousands of dollars. If there is no money, ***you get stuck with the bill.***

59. Judge versus jury

Only four to five percent (4-5%) of personal injury cases in the United States go to trial; the rest are settled beforehand. Ninety percent (90%) of personal injury cases that go to trial are lost. If you are one of the four to five percent that make it to trial, ask for a judge. ***Cases do better when the case is in front of a trial judge rather that a jury.***

60. Awards vary by state

Where you live makes a difference. For instance, Colorado is ranked 48th in awarding punitive damages. According to one attorney, everyone still considers Colorado the "Wild West" so when something bad happens, they are just supposed to "tough it out" and get on with their life.

61. Attorney fees

There are four types of payment plans:
- Hourly rate
- Flat fee
- Retainer
- Contingent fees

•Charging by the hour is the most common. Hourly fees are dependent on the location, size of law firm and experience of attorney. An attorney with a large firm in a major metropolitan city charges anywhere from $200 to $600 an hour; a small-town attorney may charge $100 to $200; an attorney who specializes in specific areas of law can command up to $1,000 an hour.

●**Flat fees** are charged when the case is simple and well defined. Examples of flat fee cases are simple wills, bankruptcy or an uncontested divorce.

●A **retainer** is an advance payment on an hourly rate case. The retainer is held in a trust account and fees and costs are deducted from it. If a client's retainer is depleted before the case closes, the attorney may request additional money before continuing work.

●When working on a **contingent fee** basis, the attorney takes no money in advance and gets paid from the money awarded. Examples of contingency cases are automobile accident lawsuits and other personal injury cases, medical malpractice and debt collection. Contingent fees are usually 33-1/3 percent if it doesn't go to trial; 40 percent if it does.

62. Handling life changes

If you suffer a permanent injury, you may have to alter how you use your body. You cannot change that, but you can control how you react. You may have to make some adaptations, but humans are good at that. Take as much time as you need, but try to move forward every day, even if it is a little bit. Things will get better. *(See #46.)*

63. Do not make comparisons

Your situation is unique. There is always going to be someone who has it worse and others who have it better. Do not compare your situation to others. Concentrate on what is best for you. *You cannot direct the wind, but you can adjust your sails.* Control what you can and let go of the rest.

64. The mouth that roared

Most people desire to be friendly. However, **sometimes people equate being friendly with being weak.** A pleasant demeanor may not be advantageous in certain situations.

For example, an agency won't release documents necessary to your case. Muster your courage. In the movie <u>We Bought A Zoo</u>, Matt Damon said: "*You know, sometimes all you need is twenty seconds of insane courage.*" Screw up your courage, turn up the volume and make yourself heard. Don't swear, don't be obnoxious, and don't threaten. Don't feel like you can do that? Invite a friend who will make your requests known without being rude.

65. Civil and criminal cases
In personal injury lawsuits, there is a possibility of two cases - criminal and civil. The differences between the two are worth further exploration.

A criminal case...

...is tried by a public attorney and sues the defendant for **any law or ordinance violated** during the commission of the incident.

...**covers out-of-pocket expenses** (medical expenses, prescriptions, co-pays, wages for people hired to do things you are unable to do - laundry, mow lawn,) etc.

...**does not allow** money awarded to be dismissed through bankruptcy.

A civil case...

...is filed by a private attorney **hired by the plaintiff.**

...covers **loss of income and pain and suffering**

...allows money awarded to **be dismissed through bankruptcy**. A person's income cannot be garnished in a civil matter.

DO YOU REMEMBER?

1. You have a better chance of taking your case in front of : a) jury b) judge c) TV court.

2. What is an easy way to find out what the statute of limitations is in your state and for your type of case?

3. Why is it a good idea to plan for the worst and hope for the best?

4. Name three differences between civil and criminal cases.

5. What is meant when a lawyer charges on a contingent basis?

8

▶RESEARCH OPTIONS

In most cases, the attorney and staff will conduct the research. However, some attorneys allow clients to help. That is good news for people who like to be involved with their case.

What type of research can you do? It depends on what the attorney is comfortable handing over to you.

66. Background check
This report contains many details that are used to ferret out other information. Your attorney can order one but you can request a report yourself. A report may include:

- Subject's name and other names used (such as maiden name)
- Social Security number (partial)
- Date of birth

- Age
- Bankruptcy
- Real estate
- Corporate affiliations (*if they are listed as a corporate officer*)
- Address summary (*current and previous, neighborhood profile*)
- Liens and judgments
- UCC Filings
- Cell phone listing
- Ranking in corporation (*if affiliated*)
- Driver's license information
- Vehicle description
- Voter registration
- Possible criminal records
- Sexual offenses
- Permits (*hunting, gun, etc.*)
- People (*not relatives*) associated with subject
- Possible relatives summary

67. Corporate affiliations

If the report indicates the person is a member of a corporation, investigate further. The Secretary of State keeps this information. You can call them directly or check their website by searching "Secretary of State *(your state)*". The website has instructions on how to search the business records. On this site you may find:

- Business Name
- Trade Name or Trademark
- Registered Agent
- Reserved Name Holder
- Trade Name Registrant
- Trademark Registrant

If your case is against the owner of a business, the person listed as the Registered Agent would be served with a subpoena or summons. If they are a registered agent for a business, perform a separate search of registered agents to see if they are the agent for other companies. *Remember, the more information you have on a person, the better.*

There may be other information available. Make and keep copies of everything.

68. Real estate ownership

Once you obtain the defendant's home address, check the assessor's records to determine if they own their home. Some states list this on line at no charge. If they do not or you can not locate it, call your county assessor to inquire how to get ownership details on a property. Anyone making mortgage payments is required to carry homeowner's insurance. This insurance could pay your medical and other expenses.

69. Renter's insurance

If the defendant rents, are they living in a large community? Many management companies require occupants to carry rental insurance which potentially could cover your costs.

70. Case information

Your attorney should keep you apprised of any court dates pertaining to your case. However, you can contact the court. Give them your case number and they will give you court dates. Ask them if you can

check your case information online.
Some courts list case information on
their website. You can plug in the
case number and see the court docket.

71. Have a back-up plan

You may encounter resistance trying
to obtain information. When Plan A
fails, try Plan B. For instance, if a city
employee balks at giving you what you
need, contact the City Council. Why?
The City Council acts as the city's
general counsel.

When contacting the City Council, go
to them in person. Let them put a face
to the voice. Phone calls are too easily
dismissed.

 BONUS ONLINE CONTENT: If you have a
problem with an insurance company, contact the
governing agency in your state. For your
convenience, find your agency here:
http://www.HowToTrainALawyer.com/Links.html.

72. Insurance problems

If you have problems with an
insurance company, contact the
regulatory agency. Every state
regulates the personal injury

insurance industry closely. For example, Indiana has a set number of days to acknowledge and respond communications. If the insurance company fails, the state will investigate and fine the company if they are at fault. When you have an issue with an insurance carrier, contact the Division of Insurance (or whatever it is called in your state).

73. Save your breath
When contacting government agencies, speak to first-tier employees only once. Request a supervisor on the next call. Management can circumvent rules; subordinates cannot.

74. Check the facts
Don't take what others say as set in stone. They may be making an educated guess or the information may have recently changed. Follow-up with a different person to see if the information is correct.

DO YOU REMEMBER?

1. If you aren't kept informed of court dates, what is another way you can find out?

2. Who should you contact if the insurance company doesn't pay a claim?

3. What are four things you can get from the Secretary of State?

4. Why is it a smart to double check research?

How To Train An Lawyer

9

▶PERSONAL SELF CARE

You may wonder why this chapter is included in a book about attorneys. Even with the best laid plans, things can go wrong. This could be the most important chapter in this book, especially if you have a personal injury case. Everyone is unique and reacts in their own way. Don't compare your situation to any other. *Do what makes you feel good and/or heal the fastest.*

75 . Accept help from others
You may be very independent, but this is a time when you should rely on others. Allow your family and friends to help. ***Be flexible in your expectations of people.*** Those who can help, will. Those who can't, may disappear for a while.

76. A sense of humor is important

When things look bleak, a sense of humor is one of your best tools. Keep friends close who have a good sense of humor. The more you look for the funny angle, the easier it becomes to find it. It is true what they say, laughter is the best medicine.

77. Focus on positive things

If you watch TV, steer clear of violent shows. Stick to funny, upbeat shows. If you like to read, pick light novels, nothing heavy. Visit museums, watch funny or light-hearted movies, eat good food. Do things that make you feel good. ***Did you know it is impossible to have two opposing thoughts at the same time?*** When you think uplifting thoughts, it is hard to have a depressing thought.

78. Be good to your body

After sustaining an injury, you may not feel hungry. But to need to help your body heal. Eat wholesome food and drink lots of water. Mix nutritious food (*feed the body*) with comfort food (*feed the mind*). Be good to yourself.

79. Therapy can help

If your emotions are running amok, get help. Don't feel like you have to tough it out by yourself. A few sessions with a therapist can help.

80. Full disclosure

When prescribing medication, the doctor will ask about allergies, vitamins or medications you currently take. The more you share, the better it will be for you. For instance, do you use caffeine? Is your stomach sensitive? Do you have problems swallowing pills? Tell your doctor as much as you can to help them make informed decisions when prescribing medication.

81. Hypnosis can help

Hypnosis is a powerful tool. It can help you gain control during stressful times. Hypnosis can lower blood pressure, reduce anxiety and speed the recovery process.

If surgery is required, ask someone to give you suggestions during the operation. When you are under anesthesia, anything you hear drops into your subconscious mind and the mind works on it to make it happen. Ask the anesthesiologist or someone else who will be present during the surgery. You could also make a tape and ask to listen to it during surgery.

 BONUS ONLINE CONTENT: To create your own healing tape to use during surgery and afterwards, download "Affirmation Rules" at SourceOfEnlightenment.com /Rules.html.

82. Medical assistants
Let doctors concentrate on taking care of your injury. Try not to take up their time with things that can be handled by others. The nurse can answer many questions. As suggested for appointments with lawyers, **have someone accompany you** on doctor visits.

83. People in the same situation
Seek out people who have experienced what you are going through. They can give you valuable insights and empathize with you.

84. Return to scene of the crime

If you were in a car accident or suffered some other injury, once you are mentally and physically able, return to the location (*if it is a safe area*). Shut your eyes and imagine taking back any power you might have lost there. One aspect of experiencing trauma is the feeling of being helpless. Taking back your power is a way to feel strong again.

85. Help others

Is there some way to share your experience with others so they can benefit from what you have gone through? Talk to groups, write a letter to the editor, write articles, call in on a radio show. Taking this kind of action helps you regain some control.

86. See the "Bigger Picture"

It is normal to think "Why did this happen to me?" We like to have answers, especially when something bad happens. You may never get an answer, but if you look for the bigger picture, it might make you feel better.

How can you see the bigger picture?

Imagine it happened to someone else. Step back and imagine the situation through someone else's eyes. What exactly happened and how has their (your) life changed since the incident?

Remove all emotion. Look at the situation like an attorney would. Write it down as you remember it. Then delete all adjectives and adverbs until you have the basics of what happened.

What did you learn? What could you share to make someone else's life better? Share what you have learned with others. You will feel better for it and they will benefit from you.

DO YOU REMEMBER?

1. Name three things you can do that will make you feel better.

2. Why should you not compare yourself to others?

3. How can you see the "bigger picture"?

4. Why is it important to talk to others who have gone through the same thing?

How To Train An Lawyer

10

►LEGAL TERMS

AKA, a/k/a, f/k/a - Also known as, formerly known as.

Arbitration - An out-of-court hearing in which a single person (or panel of attorneys and non-attorneys) not involved in the dispute will listen to you and your lawyer to help reach a solution. In binding arbitration you will have limited ability to appeal.

Attorney - A person legally appointed by another to act as his or her agent in the transaction of business, specifically one qualified and licensed to act for plaintiffs and defendants in legal proceedings. A **transactional attorney** specializes in areas of business law (contracts, real estate). A **litigation attorney** represents clients who are suing or being sued (personal injury, criminal matters).

Calendar - To assign a case a courtroom, day and time. Also refers to noting due dates of action to be taken in a case.

Civil (Case) - The private rights and remedies of men, as members of the community.

Criminal (Case) - An action, suit, or cause instituted to punish an infraction of the criminal laws.

Contingency Fee - Payment for legal services that depends, or is contingent, upon there being some recovery or award in the case. The payment is then a percentage of the amount recovered.

Defendant - The person defending or denying; the party against whom relief or recovery is sought in an action or suit.

Deposition - The testimony of a witness reduced to writing by a duly-qualified officer and sworn to by the deponent.

Discovery - In a general sense, to learn which was previously unknown; the disclosure or coming to light of what was previously hidden.

Docket - An abbreviated formal record of the proceedings in a court of justice.

Due Diligence - To investigate and evaluate a business opportunity. A general duty to exercise care in any transaction.

Interrogatories - A written question that is formally put to one party in a case by another party and that must be answered.

Litigation - A judicial controversy. A contest in a court of justice, for the purpose of enforcing a right.

Litigator - Lawyer who specializes in criminal or civil litigation.

Make You Whole - This refers to doing what is needed to make restitution, or to put the victim back to a condition where as best as possible, they haven't lost anything.

MMI - Insurance acronym referring to Maximum Medical Improvement. The point at which a medical provider determines a person's condition cannot be improved any further.

Opposing Counsel - Attorney for the other side.

Personal Injury - Personal injury law involves injury which is caused accidentally by another's failure to use reasonable care.

Petitioner - One who presents a petition to a court, officer, or legislative body.

Plaintiff - A person who brings an action; the party who complains or sues in a personal action and is named on the record.

Redacted - Censor or obscure text for legal or security purposes.

Restitution - The return of something to the owner or to the person entitled to possession. Compensation for loss.

Statute of Limitations - A federal or state law that restricts the time within which legal proceedings may be brought.

Timekeeper - A person who bills for their time on a case.

Tort - A wrong or wrongful act as distinguished from a contract.

Warrant - A document issued by a legal or government official which authorizes the police or some other body to make an arrest or search the premises.

Work Product - Notes, memoranda, writings, notes on conversations, research, and confidential materials which a lawyer has developed while representing a client, especially in preparation for trial.

ABOUT THE AUTHOR

 Ellen Hughes includes inventors Thomas Edison and Ron Popeil among people she admires. Her main creative outlet is writing, but she has dabbled with inventing, software development, and household gifts.

She started The McKee Company in 1992 as a publishing vehicle for her writings. Its tagline has been updated to "An Idea Company" to reflect the diversity of products. These products have received favorable reviews in *Readers Digest, Kiplinger Washington Letter, Denver Business Journal,* and other publications.

The McKee Company offers several products, highlighting three main ones: 1) **Office Wizard** - software template which creates a personalized office procedures manual, 2) **Adventures With Natural Healing** - book listing specifics about 27 alternative health methods making it easy to choose which one to use on health issues, and 3) **How To Train a Lawyer** - teaches people how to deal effectively with lawyers.

Visit www.TheMckeeCompany.com for more information on all the products.